WAY STATIONS

WAY STATIONS

STEPHEN GILFEDDER

RECENT
WORK
PRESS

Way Stations
Recent Work Press
Canberra, Australia

Copyright © Stephen Gilfedder, 2021

ISBN: 9780645008944 (paperback)

A catalogue record for this
book is available from the
National Library of Australia

Cover image: European Space Agency, Comet 67P. Reproduced under Creative Commons licence 2.0.
Cover design: Recent Work Press
Set by Recent Work Press

recentworkpress.com

SS

For Tess, Allie, Sam and Lara

Contents

'Everything is autobiographical and everything is a portrait...'

Lucian Freud

Captive

Checked in and speechless
Before the muted motel television
We prepared to meet the living and the dead.
Spying on your childhood, we could see
Clear across the north paddock
To the sleepout with the flypaper
Tacked along the edges of the mesh.
That night old Belvoir Lad, gelded late,
Ran the irrigation channels, roaring
And pigrooting under the freeway lights.

Undressing, you told me bedtime stories
Of his shouting till your head rang
After a bad day at the races or the trots.
To me, he was always proper and remote,
Slicked back hair and a committee badge
Looped through one lapel
And a tie no matter what occasion.
We'd just got in, I lied to your mother
The next day under prints of your father
Leading winners back to scale.

Ma could look no-one in the eye
But got her own back when he had the stroke,
Keeping him penned on the back verandah
Where he moaned like a yarded steer.
At his wake you drank with his mates, phoning
Out of the blue when the young buck son
Of the local MLA put the hard word on
That you pretended you were someone else
With a brood of kids and a psycho lover
Just not who you were, anyone in another life.

After Parthenius

Tinnitus of traffic floating in the morning swell,
I swim the septic green of the rough sea pool,
Waves slapping over iron-grouted basalt,
Pitted and razor-sharp, dissolving
Webs of foam curving from the edge.
From the windy sheds in the Twenties
Boy Charlton smeared with muttonbird oil
Stretched laps that ended in the ozone dark,
His trainer shouting splits from a fob-sourced truth.
Defined to one-hundredths, slicked and epicene
I perform stroking and tumbling from that moment
On the blocks, diving into the image of myself.

Nature Boy

Passing that forgotten turnoff
I begin the long haul back, turning
Over what was and could have been,
A sympathetic FM tuning in and out
Along glowing stands
Of canola beckoning
From scrabbled paddocks.
In the late afternoon haze headers
Work non-stop on the oil harvest,
The virgin press anointing
The shimmer of recollection,
A dead boy ever to return
At the spark of each spring season.

Questioned, locals would see
Just another of the city folk gone wrong,
A businessman in breakdown
Within a disconnected narrative,
Something about a country lad
Who killed himself, out there still
As herald to green shoots everywhere.
In truth, I didn't know him all that well,
Some second-hand knowledge of his problems,
Now just a half smile half remembered.
Yet reconstructed, the ghosts of a past life
Would gather at the abandoned car,
Marveling at the skill

Of someone on the edge
Parking right on the verge, the neatness
Of the interior, the clinically folded clothes
With drycleaning instructions
And the plastic bag of personal possessions,
Quantum of all love.

Reading the note clamped to the windscreen
'Mum, I had to go, don't worry'
And the sorry police documentation
'He was here one minute, the next
Turned into an ear of corn', knowing
That while you're never coming back,
You've never really left us here at all.

Veneration

Just days off the boat from Ireland
In the shipment of trainee priests
My father found himself in the back blocks
Near Broken Hill, carting a bore pump
From the Big Smoke during an extended dry.
Beside the driver, with the milk cans
Rattling in the back, he spotted it a mile off
Lying by the side of the road
Just near the turnoff a watchband flaring
In the sun, neatly wristed beneath a clenching fist,
Blood pumping like a water pistol
Beside the upturned Hudson Eight.
A passing cocky had used a bridle strap
For a tourniquet, and the victim
Otherwise unhurt, sat on a crate,
Cracking jokes, smoking a Craven A.
Like lost property or a slab of topside
Wrapped in *The Advocate* the severed arm
Lay in Mrs Houlahan's Coolgardie safe
For days in the outhouse above
A rammed earth floor as if waiting
For a Papal bull or miracle from Lourdes.

According to the Bishop, he was blessed
With this introduction to service in the parish
And he lasted five good years of masses,
Funerals and fundraising for the needy.
Just why he took off and joined the Air Force
In the War was never quite explained.
Growing up, we hardly talked to the Catholics
Next door and his mother back in Dublin refused
To recognize my mother or any of us kids.
On Sundays he worked in the garden
While we were packed off to Sunday School

As our neighbours piled into their baby Fiat
With their missals, practising their catechism.
Towards the end of visits to the low-church
Nursing home, whispering a *Dominus vobiscum*
His arm would raise in involuntary spasm
As he recalled the story of the severed arm
Drifting to the reliquary of the withered limb
Of Francis Xavier brought back from Goa
And paraded down the Golden Mile.

My Father Marshals the ASIO Photographers at the 1967 Referendum Rally

The shout of 'hold' seemed to come
With the shadow of a passing cloud
Somewhere from the circus
Of caravans, kombis, utes
And hand-painted panel vans.
Bled around a dust-streaked bus
A multitude pulsed, waiting for a sign,
An amoeba of students and academics,
Unionists and public servants in cardigans
On their flextime break eating
White bread sandwiches from paper bags,
Ringed by Commonwealth police.
I bought a copy of *Gurindji Blues*,
'Poor bugger me, Lord Vestey...'
The little 45 later to find
A resting place in my collection
Between The Saints and Graham Parker.
From the back of a truck
Charlie Perkins was introduced
And Ted Egan began to speak
And everything went quiet.
As the cops spread out and wedged in
Between the troublemakers and the innocents
The rhythmic chanting began and I sighted
My father in his dark glasses far at the back
Signing in mummer fashion, making
His 'ceremonial' work understood
As the photographers worked
Through the clusters, poses snapped
To last a lifetime on the files.

My Fatherland

In that foreign, half-familiar country of my childhood
Mrs Zimmermann our red-headed primary school teacher
In her cabaret dress, was 'just a refo' from war-torn Europe
Teaching the class of old and new Australians
'Mein Vater war ein Wandersmann…'.
Acting out, at 'hut,' she made us touch our heads
Me in my Fairisle sweater, Gunther in lederhosen,
Kirsti and Kristi in matching dirndl skirts and Brigitta
Fresh from the internment camp, marked and destined
To marry the man from Tom's Trash Packs
And die of cancer just after our 50th class reunion.
Turned out on parade under the eagle eye of Mr Rummery
In his blue serge suit and his ever-ready clip around the ear
For the less enthusiastic we saluted the government
Issue crates of milk curdling in the morning sun
Under a listless flag, tumbling around the playground
To the martial static of 'Sussex by the Sea'.

In a reverse migration in adolescence at Circular Quay
We clasped the spools of streamers on the SS Arcadia
As my Irish father headed to Australia House in the Strand
As the resident spook hidden behind the window displays
Of canned peaches and bronzed livesavers marching
In their modesty costumes across Bondi's golden sands.
Graduating to that English school from another age,
The bright-eyed Mr Jewitt led us through our German readers
In Gothic script with the mystery of the double 's'
Leavened with his tales of 1920s walking tours
Of the Harz, and now under an English sky, pink cheeks flaring
After cycling to school in sandals and socks, assembling
Us under the Honour Board of those who gave their lives
In two world wars spelled out in faded gold.
Exchange German teachers sang *Komm, gib mir deine Hand*
For conversation lessons on late summer evenings

In the quad, me with my disappearing Australian accent
Strolling in my prefect's paisley waistcoat,
Manufacturing those throwaway lines of refined insolence
'What do I care?... es ist mir egal ... es ist mir einerlei',
Pretending I was going somewhere in the world
Where these sorts of phrases might come in handy.

Instead it was singing German folk songs after main course
At Cooma Rotary, joining ex-Luftwaffe and Bomber Command
Crewing underground together on the Snowy
Crooning in harmony, fired by home-made rocket fuel.
Then an evening of German verse in Barkers Road
Gathered in Hilly's literary salon like old Berlin
As you shook your head at the idea of the aged-care home
Having thought you'd live at this apartment forever
After you retired from academic life.
From the entrance hall of her flat I had glimpsed
The dark eyed photographs beside her bed
The still living and always dead and you spoke of those days
Strolling along *Unter den Linden*, fingers trailing
In the waters of the *Wannsee*, not a care in the world
And then on *Friedrichstrasse* your group of friends
Approaching, and you yelling 'It's me...ich bins, ich bins...'
And they pretended not to know you, turning their faces away,
Your face still puzzled, tattoo peeping beneath the sleeve
Of your summer frock as you gifted me
A treasured volume of your beloved Schiller.

Anniversary Waltz

From the verandah the light creeps out
Another bodylength or so and then nothing
But the click and whirr of insects and the cool
Sweat patch at the hairline, the steps
Still throwing out heatwaves after midnight.

Only Barney the red heeler's company
Wrapped against the water tank corrugation
Snapping flies with a lazy head-flick
Against the backdrop of venetians
Leaking the PC's coral radiance.

The past is a shadow play of image files
Floating aimlessly across a screen
Waiting for headlights to dance across the yard,
Gravel sewing its fine arc of greeting,
Sensors tripping the light fantastic.

Tracy and the Board of Education

Years of recuperation. It could describe
The unfortunates totalling hundreds of cuts
In Brother Mulcahy's discipline book
Found under the floorboards and re-skewered
On the hook inside the senior classroom
Kept almost as it was, the crucifix
Ripped out, Latin motto painted over.

Thwack! The primeval layer of chalk
Squirts whenever repairs are made, the wood
Splinters into dust, a termite plague
Has honeycombed their vision of a farmhouse –
But at fifty bucks a week, who's counting?
Plastering against the draft, she hears
The breathing swell, pethidine click on and off.

On the third day up, a month after
The double transplant, pancreas and kidney
He's caught smoking behind the gyprock stack.
Instantly, it's Doomsday, she's on the phone
To the lawyers, then Relationships Australia.
A sucker for punishment, he comes into the light
Holding his side, takes a breath, *takes his medicine.*

The Snowline

The dog was curled
Beside the trig point cairn,
The sheltered winter sleep
Unending, the snow
Blanket drawing back.
We wouldn't even have looked
Unless your sunglasses had taken flight
As you swung around accusingly
When I trod on your heel, the frame
Skittering across the billiard balls
Of scree as we moonwalked
The sprung trail to Kosciusko.

At one point you left the mesh
To brush your legs through wildflowers
And stooped to pick a kangaroo paw
Pushing through the rock.
That first weekend reappeared
In digitised clarity, you dousing
The sauna coals, the one luxury
Appointment in the budget motel
That caught our eye from the highway.
You hadn't spoken
More than a few words

When we met the Danish students
Coming down, mocking
'Big snow, huh, quite a glacier',
Their faces painted in white
And red zinc cream flags.
Your laugh was the original
Not the recent teflon imitation,
Trilling 'It's almost summer here, you know.'
At the ski lift station there was water

Tumbling down the Funnelweb run
And you took my arm, guiding me
Around to see the frozen cluster of tourists
Under the spell of the wedgetail
Riding thermals overhead.

The Bowling Green at Night

You drive past when the timer
Switches the lights from day to night
And the hydrangeas change from blue
To puzzled black so you can wave
Goodbye to the last ghostly whites
Of the late game drinking on the terrace.

This morning on the way to work
I caught the early risers bowling
While I headed for a breakfast meeting.
The sun shadowed a nodding line
Of panamas as sprinklers dabbed out
Bias lines grooved towards the jack.

As a programmed commuter all you can
Do is return each night past the line-up
Of outdoor furniture neatly stacked,
Umbrellas furled, saluting on a job well done.
Once after a bastard of a day I went in
For a quick drink to unwind and found

Only lockers of initialled sports bags
Under dimmed security lights and the shield
Of office holders going back forever.
Leaving, the epigraph on the stucco wall
Of the groundsman's shed, tagged by the local
Signatory, ornately telling us all to get a life.

At Lunar New Year

The $25 special banquet at the China Palace
Led us to hunting on the beach
Under the stars for the lost moon.
My daughter insisted the moon was lost.
Surely the New Year couldn't start
And what year was it anyway? she asked.
Horse, Snake, Dragon?
Her grandfather tremulously
Nominated *Ox* through the grip
Of his Parkinson's as we waited
For the clouds to release the reluctant
Sliver and let us walk again.
We were not even looking at the sky
When at last a sallow crescent appeared
Miraculously at our feet
Through a dissolving filigree of foam.

From the deck the coming change
Made a night of shadow play,
With distant thunder and lightning blooms
At the edges of the sea.
Trying to speak, the southerly
Off the point sucked away our words
And in the ozone light I fancied
I could string along again
With the old man in his prime
As he juggled beer cans and crays
Outside the co-op, quoting from Hiawatha.
Hearing my brother shout
To a returning trawler at the breakwater
Before he went to Phuoc Tuy to collect
The scar tissue he carries in his head.
Imagining the rice paper wonton
At the restaurant read his words
You lucky bastards, you've got it made.

The Holiday Householder
Enters the Spirit World

In daylight, we track like detectives
For evidence, leading visitors
To the lyrebird nest, banked with mulch
And scattered with blue offertories –
Milk container lids, insulation tape
Tarpaulin from the woodpile,
A roundup of our profiles.
At night, the hen trips the security lamp
To switch on and off, transfigured
When we look to an empty pool of light.

The Soviets Reach Candelo

for Michael L'Estrange

Odd that they got so far, the clapped-out
Prefect kangaroo-hopping up that first incline
Of Brown Mountain from the long-way-around
Coast to the strip of weatherboard shops,
Windblasted paint as thin as seaspray,
Awnings jutting like an Australian jaw.

Still in their tracksuits, CCCP everymen,
Sum geographic knowledge one glance
At a confiscated map of Melbourne deemed
Illegal and the censored plan of Olympic Village
With no path leading anywhere outside.
Here revealed from the dark above the creek

A church with a priest counting funds
For the sustenance and propagation of the faith.
The shepherd, delivered, takes them to the pub
Where the town copper's hanging out betting
On the trots and the locals get the sporting guests
To demonstrate their miracle prowess

Of how through sign language with an emigree
They got the car, fixed the Southern Cross and drove.

The Piper Cherokee Comes Down Near Tilba Tilba

The sound was the ritual of clearfelling,
Kero hoiked from the back of the vintage Ferguson
Onto the mounds of grubbed stumps
Smouldering for days, to make them take.
By the time the grid had rattled
The ute's near-worn-out shockers
At the neck of the drenching paddock
There was just the metallic glow
From the far end of the strip like a roadtrain
Coming up the Tumbarumba road.
There was nothing we could do.
Closer the fencewires ran with coruscated light
With the smell of damp, seared hay.
Lance, halfway through loading cattle
Reckoned they were fishtailing in the crosswind
And made it maybe fifty feet before the stall.
Close to, a flame of galahs lifts out of nowhere,
Beating wings where sky should be.

Allie Riding Mr Gentle

My daughter on the black horse
shouting *watch me* against a landscape
with no distractions has me thinking
of another variation on the archetypal
parent theme: if only
your great-grandmother could see you now.
Fordie, the teenage jillaroo and cook
in Wild West Gippsland, rode

from Carrajung to Fish Creek in a day.
Caught in an electrical downpour,
sheltering in the cattlemen's wattle and daub
with the rammed earth floor and chooks
cooped up inside against the foxes.
Mustering, snapping out the stockwhip
like a goanna's tongue before the dismissive
stationhands, aureoled by her pride

and joy red hair, later scythed
with crutching shears when a bat
flew in her room curtained by a tarp
in the shearers' quarters and got entangled.
Giggling *If I was a horse, they'd shoot me*
in the Base Hospital, not recognizing me
but speaking to my presence as a boy.
She died light as the light-as-a-feather

cream puffs she'd bake in the speckled range
from dawn, clutching a lock of her mother's hair
and worrying about her long-dead
younger brother playing piano
in the movie palaces and sly grogs
around the year Sister Olive won the Cup.
We gathered in the crematorium
among the plastic flowers in desolate Traralgon,

cement dust from the factory floating
over the car yards and supermarkets
while the ghostly footy played out
in grey and white above her empty bed.
My daughter laughing as the big black gelding,
spooked by the wind, pigroots and kicks
against the dying day, the dying season,
hair streaming like sunlight in the sky.

Carnies

The dark was coming on
When we reached our destination,
The sweep of beach where even
Close on dusk the streaming
Wetsuits of the surf school
Pulsed like beacons in the swell.

On the rise above the sand
Caravans and a skeleton
Of the Big Top laid out on sawdust,
Guy ropes being raised by types
As leathery as the old bank managers
Forever walking on the tideline.

The performers were making up
In shadow play in backlit caravans,
As low tide became a line
Of phosphorescence, cigarettes flickering
In the dunes, murmurs from the shapes
Of hoodies, just living in the moment.

Heading back to the weekender,
Boards on top the crazy Kombi,
My son gives a magic send-off
To the carnies edging the tent upright,
Spinning wheels, grinning back at us
Clowning in a floodlit sideshow alley.

Season

Breaking from the bank
as the light got up, the foreshore
rippled with shot, tea-tree
flaring in a cordite haze.
Tussocks sponged with every step,
cold edging tidal from the ground.
It was a day for shooting things,
hollow pops and cracks came
from the marsh with its skeletons
of river gums marking the spot
where the birds would fall.
Before the opening, the guns
Had tuned up, spotlighting

rabbits, roos, magpies, starlings,
anything that moved
now pinned along the fenceline.
Through the valley of death
my bundle of rods bobbed
along the grinding shale
of the creek bed, a few early risers
hidden in damp newspaper.
In light rain, beside a hide
of Patterson's Curse, a shooter looking
like death in a four wheel drive
peered at me through wipers on delay,
open-mouthed, like a target.

The Memory Game

The way the old man told it
The posting was an endless
Diplomatic summer
With himself a central figure
In the only two towns that mattered –
Washington and New York.

Though there was decorative snow
Around Macy's and Bloomingdales
At Christmas shopping season
This merely interrupted life
In the President's box at Forest Hills
Or the compound at Hyannis Port.

Cold water flats could still be had
For a song on the Upper West Side;
Everyone ran into Cary or Barbra
Outside the 21.
Threats were just Krushchev banging
His shoe or Fidel's exploding cigars.

While Elvis had been made a production line
Ranks of ICBMs
In Westchester county still pointed East.
You thought all I would remember
Was playacting kookaburras and kangaroos
To ingratiate with my elite classmates.

But I have surviving evidence,
A collection of whitening polaroids, groups
Of sunglassed men in reflective polyester suits
Outside anonymous Government facilities
And you in a barbecue apron whirling a martini tray
At the Consulate cocktail party.

We know it ended not when you said
When Kennedy was shot
Or even when 'those Beatles'
Appeared on coathanger Mr Ed
But with your spin and crash before retirement
From your first angina on the Beltway.

The Criminology Students Visit the Youth Offenders Portables

Berrima Gaol, 1968

A cubby house production line, two by two
In neat stepped rows between the sandstone,
Two to cottage, behind the buffed stoops
And brass numbers, locked at seven every night
Without power in a subzero highland freezer.
Even at midday, permafrost covers the shingle roofs,
Walls as big as Crackenback, impossible to climb.
A whistle leads us to the young thrill-riders
And carnal knowledge kings barely shaving,
Standing as invisibly as possible beside neatly folded
Army blankets, tatts creeping from faded Chesty Bonds.
Their rooms are a riot of Elvis, gilt crosses,
Messages to mothers crafted in the rehab block,
Pin-ups and pictures of great escape V8s.
Everywhere two lists, the Crimes Act framed like family
And house rules under plastic, no fighting, sex or drugs.
Like criminals, we slip each kid the smuggled cigarettes.
The culpable driving junior league player blows a kiss.

Backgrounder on the Grand Champignon, Australian Mushroom Show

Last of the line, I'm elbow deep
in the old machinery shed, surrounded
by polystyrene boxes, spores and compost,
keeping an eye out for the Ag Department rep
waging war on unregistered production.
The secret's to be positive, set goals
according to that personal development
magazine I get monthly (part-funded
by rural industries training and research).
The family if they were here would back
me up, but our history wouldn't.
Warren walked into the open septic
at his twenty-first; it'd just been pumped
and Cec forgot to put the lid back on.
Cec baled himself slipping off the combine
taking the last of the winter wheat
and young Maurie went swimming in the silo;
Darryl's a presence in every Asian feedlot.
The female line extinct, Esme about to marry
old grazier stock, blood poisoned by her appliqué.
Working blind, feeling for the cups that might
just be pushing through, I check for signs of life.

Site Inspection

With my fast food lunch and mobile
I climb the hill where I used to park
the car with Margaret, now the psychologist
working with the anxious and depressed.
I skirt the clusters of honeyeaters hanging
from red and yellow cotoneaster berries
among the tent pegs and survey tape
of the new townhouse development.

Shadowing the cyclone fence,
I follow the trail of renewal,
past crushed cigarette packets
and cans and faded soft porn
magazines caught in the net.
A wind song courses through the wire
along plumblines of trenches carved
among the heritage-protected gums.

I find the spot beside the rock, grass flattened
by the westerly which has blown all week
under a site board where a Minister smiles
over initials which cannot be forgotten.
Trail bikes wheel across the rise
bringing a squall of cockatoos
and a hoarding of memory.
In the rear vision mirror reversing out
a weathered face covers the landscape.

That Second Honeymoon

Around three in the morning
a metallic shower sweeps the roof
and I sleep walk to the deck,
in the spotlit ceremony of retrieving
beach towels and evidence
of other pleasures left to dry.
For adult viewers out this late
my naked raindance, pointless
and unchoreographed, while
behind the glass you are composed
holding on to life with a sheet
screwed tight in your fist.
Outlined as the victim of love
one arm trails to the holiday reading
of the solitary, hard-boiled cop
discarded after a dozen pages,
spine spent, the crime unsolved.
I remember from the blurb
He watched her at a distance
through the window
knowing her every move
as I come back to you, snapping
the sliding door, leaving footprints
on the carpet, searching for clues
on where we go from here.
I guess that in the morning
when it clears we'll see the path
we walked today through the tangle
of bush to the sea's inviting edge.
For a dozen years of marriage
we have looked at views like this,
holding on to our younger selves,
uncertain of what we have become
and what we're guilty of.

The Origins of Ornithology

Milk was ladled into the billy can
Sitting on the letterbox, you left
The doily with the beads on top
And scooped the cream off with a spoon.
Mr Currie, our dentist, cycled through the fog
To take out my impacted wisdom teeth
The same weekend that Mrs Hebden
After a shandy in the two-tone FC
Outside the beer garden at the Ainslie Rex
Took an axe to her old man, the spec painters
Using five coats to finalise divorce.
She was a queer old bird, my mother said.

Waiting on contracts for the Snowy
The German boys looked after our Tocumwal
For Christmas while at the coast we joined
Kids from the Far West Children's Home
Leaping on consignment in the surf.
A fairytale cuckoo clock was left
Wrapped in *Neue Welt* on the kitchen table,
An envelope of notes weighed down with *stollen*.
The morning after buying the Muscovy fleet
We heard the uplift beating, reaching
The verandah just in time to see the big V
Dipping in farewell, wings unclipped.

My father stood the old fruit box
On its end and planted his gumboot
On the rooster's neck, the comb
Buried in the peacock shimmer.
The box fell like a guillotine
Before the axe neatly flipped the head
With its opaque eye into the gully trap.
Lifting the box too soon the headless

Chook chased me along the neat rows
Of vegies, a free-range avenging angel.
Left hanging in the toolshed, stray feathers
Wound down like tears day by day.

My father recited Heraclitus
To the solemn immigrants from Kythera
After Suzie came back from the Olympic Pool
And died that night of Golden Staph.
My mother stoked the speckled range
With the blackened jemmy in the lid
A tea towel bandanna around my shoulders
And my father ran the home hairclippers
Up my neck, pinning my ears,
Gauging the collar line with his thumb,
Under the cuckoo clock wedged
With dowel, songless on the mantelpiece.

On the Numeralla

My brother casts the blue-eye
spinner, floating it over the sheet calm
on the upside of the spillway, an act
of levitation to dragonflies cruising
islands of reeds for early risers.
He wears the waders I've never worn,
admired in the *Weekly Times* and gifted
to me on changing jobs with Grange
cravatted in Buck's ties, one each boot.
(The wine long gone on family celebrations,
he borrowed their outer wrapping
for 'just a day or two, in case they fit').
Crutch-deep, he's legless in reflection,
younger than his fifty years, in a gorge
too far removed from any useful hospital,
the edict not to travel more than fifty kays
from stocks of plasma based on the seven
packs he got through in a night at Calvary.
A fair collection of symptoms his legacy
from Vietnam but recognition too – TPI Veteran,
on delegations to the Minister, for his mates
he headed the contingent in the March.
Now he's into simpler things, getting
back to what maybe never was but what
he'd like to be, twisting the peacock lure,
leading old diggers to the shrine in Binalong.

Painting Class

for my brother, Major Dan

With the night coming on and the cool change
I sit on the back steps with the cigarette
I'm not allowed to have inside and watch
my neighbour up against the penumbral moon,
spraypainting his roof a newer shade of green,
the backpack hunched against the roofline.

Balanced on the ridgecapping a cassette
plays vintage Stones above the unearthly blue
flicker of the television in the lounge,
keeping his spellbound wife below.
He moves the wand back and forth, healing
the crazed surface, his face rendered
expressionless in the moonlight,
younger or as if he could be anyone.

Night is the best time to spread things around
- the agent orange decanted from the fluorescent 44s
the Pasture Improvement Society sprayed
perfectly onto the grid of Phuoc Tuy Province,
the invisible rain falling gently
from the Huey's pods into the black below
where you just couldn't see results
and you took them for the best.

Keep out of sunlight he says,
though doctors believe it would do him good
and night he reckons is not the time to dream,
it all comes back, with his tell tale
face and hands covered in psoriasis,
some sort of sentence for the guys who went.
But I figure he should be able to feel
the day's last warmth stuck to the buckle

of the corrugated iron and see the light
concentrated for him in one corner of the sky,
a kind of lurid advertising hoarding
of what the real thing could be like.

Later the Friday night ritual has him sit
in the yellow square of the kitchen and get down
the inscribed and crested pewter mugs
to have with the take-away from the Nui Dat,
wearing the corps tee shirt and his old army shorts,
after he's painted it all back, dog tags glinting,
under the blips of the commuter choppers
flying from the heliport at Mascot.

Crime Scene

for the late Stan and Esme Livingstone,
suspected of murdering Margaret Clement for
her property 'Tullaree' in Gippsland, Victoria

Esme and Stan could not be real life
murderers, more like the creation
of a 50s noveliste with a nom-de-plume.
I can remember the bright and jerky
Super Eight of me swinging
on the apple tree with the toothpaste grin
and the decorative couple leaning
on the gate smiling with my dad
in the shadow of Uncle Alf's long pan.
Stan's brilliantined brushback
shone beside Esme's slash of lipstick,
as lush as a barmaid's, her face
a changing patchwork of light and leaves.
Around the old upright at night
the ice clinked in the Johnnie Walker
as my parents sipped cream sherries
before the production cut through the years
and their sober reappearances
from London exile at coronial inquiries
whenever Aboriginal bones were found
as the Shire Council drained the swamp.
On my eighth birthday I walked with Stan
on an inspection of the irrigation channels
carrying Miss Clement's stick to carve
through the bullgrass and wallop
any tiger snakes that crossed our path.
Sporting a Jermyn Street panama,
with Esme's perfume swirling around me,
he checked the new electric fence
I dared myself to touch and felt
the low voltage rumble through my veins
all the while watching such innocent eyes.

Collective

You cannot imagine said Dr Opek
from the verandah of his weatherboard
at the end of Busby Street the scale of deportations.
Twenty years in Shanghai had distilled a double exile,
he spoke a form of diplomatic English
manufactured at a language school in Moscow.
He could recall little Riga, the Unter den Linden
barracks and the Crimean quarter in Vladivostok,
German POWs hauling lumber on the ice,
blond Ukrainians in the forests.
He was never where he was, always
in another country recalling somewhere else.

Returning from exile, I pull up in a cab
from the airport on an overnight business trip
and document the dead square
where the pigeon loft has been removed
and the dacha colours on the guttering
and window trim stripped and varnished.
My mother serves the last old boiler
From the chook run and at eight she goes to bed
with the radio and a crocheted hot water bottle
under the twinned pictures
of Our Lord and Mal Meninga.

I squeeze into my childhood bed and gulp
the miniature scotches scored on business class
for occasions such as this,
primed for the early morning wake-up call.
Instead I end up with tartars in a long train
of open-topped mini-cars like a scenic railway,
sitting four by four in the warm open air,
flaps of astrakhan hats turned up,
boots and gold teeth gleaming.
The track barrels straight through endless tundra
miraculously transported under southern stars.

When the train stops in the middle
of nowhere I escape unnoticed
by simply stepping into the landscape.
The last cars move past silently
followed by the fading pulse of a cigarette
held by a solitary guard,
singing a sad song of Mother Russia.
At first light I run, clambering over cyclone fences,
suburban backyards, Hills Hoists, barbecues,
above ground pools and wattles in bloom,
everything I cannot imagine.

Weather Eye

I scrabble under the withered stalks
for the bulbs to break their spines,
calculating next year's number
from the resonating plastic buckets.

They have rest to look forward to,
to just being in the neglected dark
of the garage, hanged in hessian bags
from butcher's hooks, their names

chalked above them on the gyprock.
All seasons my father worked the beds
but it doesn't show, the lot gone wild
through neglect and the unforgiving soil.

Strange combinations. Potatoes
introduced to breach the clay have seeded
among grevilleas and these contorted fingers
entwined like dad's towards the end.

Every year I allocate a single day
to his lifetime's work, holding
the reclusive almanacks, turning them
over and over, looking for the best

division along the seasons of scar tissue.
On the cold cement floor with its imprint
of dead leaves I arrange the tools
I will need in winter to dig them in.

Lunchtime at Harden Abattoirs

for Bernie Newell

The shiftworkers have walked across the road
from the abattoir in their lunch break
to the wheatfield neatly shaved to stubble
to play the real game, rugby league,
no touch football or that poofter
southern code round here.
The crows cry over this dusty paddock
in the back blocks, as if they care.
Circular hay bales are rolled up
to mark the goal posts and overalls
are discarded for the try line.
The foreman and union rep is given the whistle,
told that's all he's good for,
and there is a moment when the ball is kicked
when everything is still
and you can hear the sound of air in air
before Chicka and company begin
shuddering into each other
like great sides of beef and the scrum
forms with a collective sigh
fighting over one small patch of ground.
You cannot see the ball.
The driver of the refrigerated roadtrain
keeps time and sounds the halves
through his double air horns,
the continuous airconditioning humming
like an expectant crowd.
Killing halal for the export trade
the resting imam's agent with the blue stamp
stands in a bloodied surgical smock
making up the spectators with my son and me
watching from the cattle ramp.
In the background the processing continues

with the carry-over shift, we hear the regular
clubbing of the electric stun gun
and the screech like chalk on a blackboard
where the carcases are marked up.
The semis continue to ferry in
their cargo pressed tight against the bars,
the back bred baldies watching their jailers
at play in what was their domain.
The men gather round a dying form,
the koori prop forward lying stunned
on the red dirt among the straw,
arms and legs in spasm,
his mouthguard an agonized minstrel whiteface
in the cursory ritual of checking him out.
My son swoops on the unattended ball
and throws me the perfect pass
as the number thirteen laughs it off,
limping back to position, testing on the way
that the sidestep is still there
while I sign off the cattle.

Leaving the Coffin House, Nantucket

The deckhand dances with the reins of rope
and guides the gangway into the mouth
of the ferry wall one-handed,
balancing with the other the boombox
on his shoulder bleating
Miles Runs the Voodoo Down.
'Hey, Aussie, I know you,
say that thing again'.
He talks through his cigarette,
each word a smoke ring
merging with another.
I make him laugh
just by opening my mouth.
We join the others in claiming seats,
and steam like clams in our hooded jackets,
ridiculous beside our bags
representing people.
Our white breath billows in the ice blue cabin,
a convention of journeyman fire eaters
shuddering into the late fall grey.
The ferry slices the fluted waves
running off Great Point down to Siasconset
and Mrs Richard Lovelace shakes my hand.
Mr Lovelace's moon face smiles
through half moon glasses
over the paper on semiconductors
he's working on for MIT.
When he snaps his briefcase shut
I am jerked from napping to see the moving picture
of the deckside constitutional,
the headscarved lookalikes
fists pumping, leaning like ski-jumpers,
a row a Pulcinella cheeks
rouged by the wind blowing off the Cape.

The flimsy summer houses are left
like latticed driftwood on the harbour shore
and we run the sewerage trails,
the aftermath of Hurricane Bob,
pumping out from flooded cellars
the drowned collections
floating just beneath the surface,
little memories trying to peer into our lives.
Last night jet-lagged I drowned my sorrows
with too much duty free.
Not much of a drinker
I blacked out beneath the stars
trompe l'oeiled on the ceiling
of the Queequeg Room.
Rigidly awake an hour later
beside my sleeping wife and child
I finished the bottle reading
Costner's History of Whaling in Massachusetts
placed Gideon-like beside the bed
with its hand-tinted lithographs
of the lurid dockside cauldrons
melting down the chunks of flesh,
the torrents of steaming whale oil
anointing the navvies
who stoked the fiery furnace
and the children lowered to cut the blubber
inside the bellies of the beasts
posed like angelic Jonahs between the jaws.
On deck through the snowstorm
of next morning's hangover
my daughter mouths incomprehensibly
through the steamed up porthole
a mermaid imprisoned in a tank
and the ferry repeats the flat goose bark
looking for its kind on the petrified water.
Mrs Lovelace talks of deformed lobsters
missing claws from New York

dumping garbage off the continental shelf
and passes binoculars for me to see
Balaena Mysticetus,
a hundred yards across the Sound
the spume of the rare Greenland Right
cow and calf migrating north.

Parkinson's

Standing in the garden at some unearthly hour
my ghostly presence unannounced
having coasted the car
ignition off into the garage,
my head clears in the suburban silence
of the Canberra midwinter chill
as clinical as pethidine.
I watch the vapour trail
of the northbound pre-curfew unwind
through the smeared clusters of the heavens
the plane and its compliant cargo invisible,
carried to a bright awakening,
my breath floating in clouds beneath them.
When last I played among the stars
I was at the half-yearly sales conference
trapped pre-dawn with Bernie
at the heliport the nav lights whirling
off our frozen faces.
We rode in Bell Jetrangers line abreast
across the Whitsundays
into the first sun splintering on the perspex,
emerging bit by bit
like ashen Tiwi birdmen
buzzing the pontoons and reefs
our shadow racing with the marlin
in the shallow corridors of coral
until I was sick and lay
as if dead under the wet towel on the beach
the pilot intoning his apologies beside me.

Entering the house black with mourning
I am the grim reaper with my father's belongings
in the first of vinyl airline bag
and hear the soft striking

of my daughter's asthmatic cough
floating in the dark.
It is projected as full
and from the diaphragm
as her music teacher has her sing
the endless rounds of scales,
with the same waiting
for the sequence to fail.
I cannot even whistle
The cartoon tunes right through,
without her stopping me to laugh
and pitching the note
like a small balloon for me to touch.
I track to her room by the nightlight
hovering above her head,
my wife sleeping with her on the Disney bed
the faces myopically replicated
on the pillow.
My father sits beside them
in his flying jacket and neat moustache.
For the past excised year
I have placed the same plastic mask
on the old airman's face
in the half-light diorama
of the nursing home
as he struggled to take in breath
from the metal tank of oxygen,
his withered arm in tremens
beckoning me closer.
Now I wear his coat
and fold a final bus ticket
from the pocket for the limpid child,
guiding her head
to ride into the healing clouds.

Jockeys at St Kilda Pier

They float
like ghosts of children
in the hot sea bath
the Sunday after the races.
Thin white arms
flap ineffectually against the steam
and transparent faces
turn to the stranger
for affirmation of their denial.
Today they will barely eat or drink.
Yet those delicate wrists
have the power to make or break
larger men and their happiness.
A few have perfected
smoking on their backs,
cigarettes held above the water,
beacons in the sulphurous gloom.
The sinewy bodies nose and bump,
each tragically mirrored to twice its size.
Earlier they could have been mistaken
for dancers in their Italian shoes,
prancing onto the pier
from imported limousines.
Rubbing down, the retired hoop
slaps red whip marks
on the skinny frames
and with a final drum roll
sends them to the sauna.
Their wish is to become still smaller.

The Munitions Divers

for James Joseph Gilfedder
killed in action
May 31, 1916

Three blasts from the whistle
starts a crazy dance
of wheelchairs spinning
in the summer heat.
On leave from their nursing homes
the two surviving widows, ninety-odd,
are anchored by their bags of duty free.
(Why shouldn't old women
have Givenchy and Johnnie Walker Black?).
They manoeuvre the wreath
from reluctant relatives
over the sliprail
onto the shifting, oily sea.
The ferry circles once
and heads from the Jutland Bank,
riding the current back to Hartsholm.

Beneath a sky like white-out
the North Sea curls
and breaks its tremulous green
among the tufted hillocks
and the twisted bracken
where thick-necked horses
are turned to pasture.
When we dock clutching each other
spray from the surging undertow
is splashed across our faces
like holy water
as the ship's bell rings.
The buoys of the lobster pots
dribbling tears of rust

pitch and swell in line.
All night from the guesthouse
We hear the yawning cast of the anchor chains
Pulling at the changing tide.
Restless at the window
I see you bobbing white
Against the phosphorescent sea.

Old Mr Olsen who holds the keys
of the Municipal Museum
opens the unfrequented schoolhouse
on the quay as promised on the sign outside
'By appointment, Tuesdays and Fridays only.'
He stands like an exhibit in the half-light
among the display cases of the past.
He spreads his hands.
All thanks to the co-operative he says.
From an English transcript stapled to the handbook
he recites that the coast was famous for its wrecks.
The locals gathered everything washed ashore:
the sea-turned wood became an architrave,
exotic fruit were soaked in akvavit,
a crate of best burgundy
was hoarded for Midsummer Night.
Cottages were ornamented with the wrack
and families photographed with their trophies –
a horn of ivory, a Parisian mode.
Coconuts husks were painted
and lined the window sills.
From winter to winter the dead grey sea
Rolled back to leave among the harvest
The unknown sailors buried on the headland.

'Here I am as a baby with my parents.'
Mr Olsen points at the black-clothed figures
Standing on the causeway at low tide.
'Behind us you see the shapes

of the sailors from the great battle.
The village worked for weeks to bury them.'
Out in the sunlight
we climb the hill and inspect
the rows of regulation graves,
German and British lying together.
Along the cliff top
the Scandanavian nudists stand
in Walkmans and sunglasses
watching the arrival of the dive launch
with its catch of copper cable
and brass shell casings.
All week the dull tremor
of detonations out to sea
has resonated the Heineken sign
outside the hotel bar,
a shimmering wind song for the dead.

Rolling his wetsuit to his waist
Irish Dave taps out his pipe
against the wire cage of salvage.
Sponging encrusted salt
from the lycra he spreads
an Admiralty map
and pinpoints boilers, funnels, twelve-inchers,
the shattered hulls with their invisible crews,
spread along the narrow channel.
The reclaimed metal ashtray souvenirs remain unsold.
His Rolex fires tracers in the sun.
He speaks of waking in the night
believing he has drowned,
the off-season on the reef,
siren brown women,
and the cathedrals of coral
where a man can lose himself.

Laying the Cat's Eyes

At a distance backed up we hear
the dull stamp
of the feeder.
Then the roadman swivels
his sign to go
and only then we see
the task at hand.
Two reflectors equidistant
laid perfectly in rows
twenty metres apart.
It requires an elemental skill:
we are talking about an exact
twenty metres repeated
to get that nighttime filigree
running through the dark.
Passing the crew at speed
we salute our thanks.
They do not look up.
For every one of us
there's another stretch of road
and targets to be reached.
We are measured simply
in bins of sparkling jewels.
Picnicking miles away we hear
the lumbering engine
catching up
planting its sightless eyes.

Ghost Story

When we do not look
they gather
in the echoing hallway
and the darkened rooms
in the stifling town
at midday.
From the breathless curtains
swells the reedy organ
and the flickering shadows
of the long-departed
television program and its American host.
There is the emphysemic cough
and the shuffling slippers
and those certain loving phrases
repeated only for our benefit.
They are mouthing in coral light
for us to visit
at Christmas, Easter,
each and every birthday.
Endlessly, they come to us
in dreams
writing cards, sending invitations,
willing us to appear.
I pretend I am in contact
across the void,
eyes closed, my hands fleshed
upon the table.
Vibrating cutlery, rattling china
I hold my breath.
Things move into place.
You look at me and break the spell.
'You grow more like your father every day.'

Going Over It Once Again

Outside in the winter trees
a pair of sulphur-crested cockatoos
have watched all week
with impenetrable eyes
from the stripped branches.
Over the landscape
nothing moves, the sky dissolves
and dissolves its watery film
as far as the eye can see.
I wander from room to room
drinking to absent friends.
On the dark side of the house
Frost melts on a green face of moss.

In the backyard
sheltered from the sun's pale light
the lawn has browned and died.
As featureless as the room
where Dave's friend Frank
shrank to nothing in a cancerous bed.
Walking on the sodden leaves
turning into earth
I think of the few jokes
I told last night against the news.
In the glowing house I hear singing
and see my daughter trace
a stick figure on the clouded window.

Prawning

In the night above a plane
bears its three stars
through a starless sky
the hollow sound moves westward
under a diaphragm of clouds
a furred sliver of moon
across the bay the wind
scuds in lines shivering
and snapping our shirts and shorts
a fine salt hail pinches the skin
there must be thirty of us
standing in the shallows
like sentinels our gas lamps burning
pale stars in the black water
our nets raised like prosthetic arms

for a while we talk
our faces expressionless
as stocking masks in the soft light
then grow quiet waiting for the run
we spread out wading slowly
trailing streamers of dazzling foam
our hands glow
white and effeminate
as surgeons' under the operating lamps
some rock cod dart away
their delicate mouths kissing the water
like distracted lovers
then a series of sand puffs at my feet
I use my net
and throw the clockwork catch
to Charlie, who holds the sack

Under the Flightpath

The summer night was light with stars
and the warm air floated
wattle pollen on the sill
yellowing my hands
as I brushed the burrs in little heaps
you could feel the dark
gathering inside the house
the earth smell from the garden
and tight fists of petals
their chemical breath
heat rising from the walls

from next door voices carried
a man cried
I ought to beat the living Christ out of you
the words rang briefly in the night
and disappeared
making no sound
I followed a delicate red pulse
along the flightpath
Leonardo's inheritors circled my heart
messages in their plumed trails
and cargoes of fixed smiles
being brought to earth

changing on the bed in the half-light
you played with your nipples
until you shivered drawing up a sheet
and talked about your husband
rings and ceremonies
their significance to others
and how you didn't need such things

Author's Note

These poems were written over a period of more than forty years. Necessarily, the language reflects the times in which they were written, and some words, spellings and sayings may be considered these days archaic or even inappropriate. Nevertheless, the poems aim to portray the lives of individuals at moments in time, unfiltered, in their inherited and created environments and the circumstances that confront them.

Acknowledgements

The poems in this collection have been published variously in *Quadrant, The Weekend Australian, Westerly, Island, The Canberra Times, The Sydney Morning Herald, The Australian's Review of Books, Imago, Newcastle* and *Mattara Poetry Prize* anthologies, and *Poetry Australia*.

About the Author

Stephen Gilfedder was born in Melbourne in 1948. After secondary schooling in England, he was further partially educated at the Australian National University and the University Of Melbourne. He has worked variously as a mail sorter, storeman, travelling salesman, journalist, public servant, Ministerial private secretary, as media, public relations and marketing managers, advertising executive, and government relations consultant. His first published poem was in 1970 and since then he has published widely in literary journals, periodicals, newspapers and anthologies of new and prize verse.

9 780645 008944